Torque brims with excitement perfect for thrill-seekers of all kinds. Discover daring survival skills, explore uncharted worlds, and marvel at mighty engines and extreme sports. In *Torque* books, anything can happen. Are you ready?

This edition first published in 2024 by Bellwether Media, Inc.

No part of this publication may be reproduced in whole or in part without written permission of the publisher. For information regarding permission, write to Bellwether Media, Inc., Attention: Permissions Department, 6012 Blue Circle Drive, Minnetonka, MN 55343.

Library of Congress Cataloging-in-Publication Data

Names: Moening, Kate, author.
Title: The Cold War / by Kate Moening.
Description: Minneapolis, MN : Bellwether Media, Inc., 2024. | Series: Torque : War histories | Includes bibliographical references and index. | Audience: Ages 7-12 | Audience: Grades 4-6 | Summary: "Engaging images accompany information about the Cold War. The combination of high-interest subject matter and light text is intended for students in grades 3 through 7"– Provided by publisher.
Identifiers: LCCN 2023007741 (print) | LCCN 2023007742 (ebook) | ISBN 9798886874525 (library binding) | ISBN 9798886875447 (paperback) | ISBN 9798886876406 (ebook)
Subjects: LCSH: Cold War–Juvenile literature. | World politics–1945-1989–Juvenile literature. | United States–Foreign relations–1945-1989–Juvenile literature. | Soviet Union–Foreign relations–1945-1991–Juvenile literature.
Classification: LCC D843 .M645 2024 (print) | LCC D843 (ebook) | DDC 909.82/5–dc23/eng/20230221
LC record available at https://lccn.loc.gov/2023007741
LC ebook record available at https://lccn.loc.gov/2023007742

Text copyright © 2024 by Bellwether Media, Inc. TORQUE and associated logos are trademarks and/or registered trademarks of Bellwether Media, Inc.

Editor: Elizabeth Neuenfeldt   Designer: Josh Brink

TABLE OF CONTENTS

WHAT WAS THE COLD WAR?	4
GROWING DISTRUST	6
THE ARMS RACE BEGINS	8
STRUGGLES IN EASTERN EUROPE	14
THE SOVIET UNION FALLS	18
GLOSSARY	22
TO LEARN MORE	23
INDEX	24

WHAT WAS THE COLD WAR?

The Cold War lasted from 1947 to 1991. It was between the United States and the **Soviet Union**. The U.S. had a **democracy**. The Soviet Union had **communism**.

Each side feared the other was too powerful. They never fought directly. But they helped opposing sides in other wars. They also built **nuclear weapons**. They feared nuclear war.

NUCLEAR BOMB GOING OFF

COLD WAR ALLIANCES IN 1962

NATO member = ◆   Warsaw Pact member = ◆

COLD WAR ALLIES

Both sides had allies. In 1949, the U.S. joined NATO. This allied it with 11 countries. The Soviet Union later allied with 7 nations. This was the Warsaw Pact. In time, more alliances formed.

GROWING DISTRUST

In 1945, **World War II** ended. The U.S. helped Europe rebuild. Meanwhile, Joseph Stalin led the Soviet Union. He made communist governments in Eastern Europe. This worried the U.S. Soon, the Cold War began.

In 1949, Germany split in two. It became a center for the war. East Germany and the Soviet Union were **allies**. West Germany sided with the U.S.

JOSEPH STALIN

BERLIN WALL CONSTRUCTION

EAST AND WEST GERMANY

East Germany
East Berlin
West Berlin
West Germany

East Germany = ◆
West Germany = ◆
Berlin Wall = ◆

THE BERLIN WALL

Berlin was an important city in the war. It split when Germany split. In 1961, East Germany built a wall around West Berlin. It kept people from fleeing East Germany.

THE ARMS RACE BEGINS

The U.S. first used a nuclear weapon in 1945. The Soviet Union wanted to keep up. They tested one in 1949. Soon, the **arms race** began. Both sides built more powerful weapons. In time, nuclear **missiles** could travel across oceans.

THE SOVIET UNION'S FIRST NUCLEAR TEST

In 1952, the U.S. also tested a **hydrogen bomb**. It was 1,000 times more powerful than earlier bombs!

THE FIRST HYDROGEN BOMB

Size of mushroom cloud:
100 miles (160.9 kilometers) wide and over 22 miles (35.4 kilometers) high

Weight of bomb:
82 tons
(74.4 metric tons)

Energy produced:
10.4 megatons
of energy

The two countries fought in **proxy wars**. These wars took place around the world. One was the **Vietnam War**.

Both sides also spied on each other. The U.S. and the Soviet Union created large spy groups. Spies gave leaders secret information about their enemies. Leaders learned about enemy military plans.

○ VIETNAM WAR ○

RADIO FREE EUROPE

Soviet leaders tightly controlled news in Eastern Europe. The U.S. secretly used radio to share news in Eastern Europe. They hoped to get people to protest communism.

★ THE WAR AT HOME ★

The U.S. planned for a nuclear attack. Many bomb shelters were built in the 1950s and 1960s. They were under the ground.

Children practiced nuclear safety drills at school. Many books and movies during this time were about nuclear war.

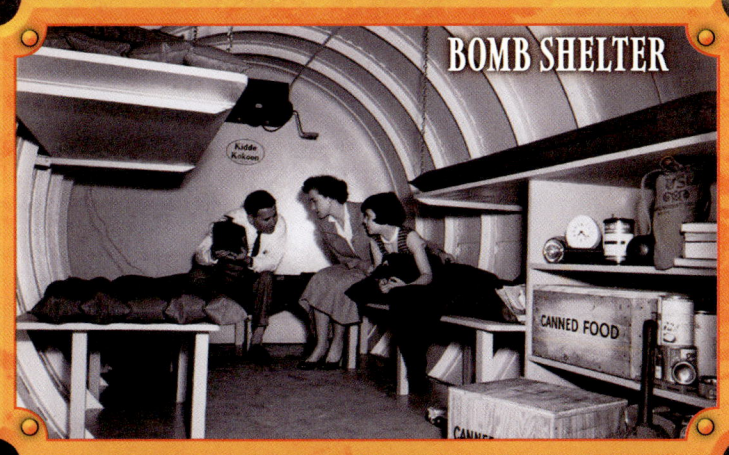

BOMB SHELTER

The Cuban Missile Crisis happened in 1962. Nuclear war nearly broke out. U.S. spies saw nuclear weapons in Cuba. The Soviets had placed them there. The U.S. feared an attack.

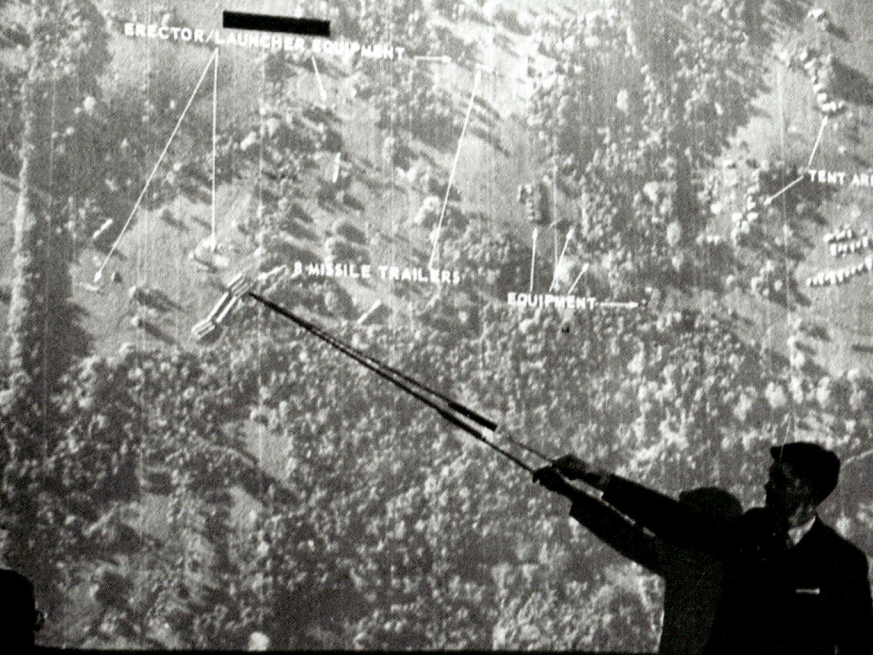

THE CUBAN MISSILE CRISIS

U.S. COLD WAR LEADER

NAME
John F. Kennedy

NATIONALITY
American

POSITION
U.S. President (1961 to 1963)

IMPORTANT ACTIONS
- 1961: Sent more U.S. troops and spies for the Vietnam War

- 1962: Helped end the Cuban Missile Crisis

- 1963: Signed a treaty with the Soviet Union and the United Kingdom to limit nuclear weapon tests

President John F. Kennedy met with Soviet leaders. Weeks later, they made peace. Soviet leaders removed the missiles. The U.S. agreed to not attack Cuba.

STRUGGLES IN EASTERN EUROPE

Tensions eased in the late 1960s and 1970s. The U.S. and the Soviet Union signed new **treaties**. They agreed to not help other countries build nuclear weapons. They agreed to limit long-range nuclear missiles.

THE U.S. AND THE SOVIET UNION SIGNING A TREATY

THE SPACE RACE

Both sides also raced to get into space. The Soviet Union got there first in 1961. In 1969, the U.S. put the first person on the moon.

But by the 1980s, the Soviet Union was in trouble. Supplies were low. People did not have enough money. They struggled to live.

In 1985, Mikhail Gorbachev came to power in the Soviet Union. He wanted to make the Soviet Union stronger. He began to open the **Iron Curtain**. He loosened Soviet borders. He worked more with the U.S.

MIKHAIL GORBACHEV WITH U.S. PRESIDENT RONALD REAGAN

SOVIET COLD WAR LEADER

NAME
Mikhail Gorbachev

NATIONALITY
Soviet

POSITION
General Secretary of the Communist Party of the Soviet Union (1985 to 1991); President of the Soviet Union (1990 to 1991)

IMPORTANT ACTIONS
- 1987: Signed a treaty with the U.S. to take apart some nuclear missiles
- 1989: Let Eastern European countries form their own governments
- 1991: Stepped down as leader of the Soviet Union

Gorbachev allowed more democracy in Eastern Europe. But people wanted more freedom. They held large **protests**.

THE SOVIET UNION FALLS

In November 1989, there was a big protest. At least 500,000 people gathered in East Berlin. Soon after, many went to the Berlin Wall. They tore it down.

This event sparked change. Germany became one nation again. Eastern European countries became more free. The Soviet Union began to fall apart.

COLD WAR TIMELINE

August 1949
The Soviet Union tests its first nuclear weapon

1940s and 1950s
The U.S. and the Soviet Union form new alliances with other European nations

October 1962
The Cuban Missile Crisis takes place

THE BERLIN WALL BEING TORN DOWN

July 1, 1968
The U.S. and the Soviet Union agree to not help other countries build nuclear weapons

November 9, 1989
The Berlin Wall begins to fall

December 25, 1991
Gorbachev steps down and the Soviet Union breaks up

On December 25, 1991, Gorbachev stepped down. The Soviet Union broke up. In its place, 15 countries formed. Russia was the largest. The U.S. and Russia began to limit nuclear weapons. The Cold War was over.

Today, tensions between the U.S. and Russia are high. But the end of the Cold War created a few years of peace.

★ BY THE NUMBERS ★

1,000,000 U.S. people = 👤   1,000,000 Soviet Union people = 👤

CASUALTIES IF NUCLEAR WAR HAD BROKEN OUT (1968 ESTIMATE):

- U.S.: **134** million
- Soviet Union: **140** million

ORIGINAL NATO MEMBERS (U.S. ALLIES):

- **12** Belgium, Canada, Denmark, France, Iceland, Italy, Luxembourg, the Netherlands, Norway, Portugal, the United Kingdom, the United States

WARSAW PACT MEMBERS (SOVIET ALLIES):

- **8** Albania, Bulgaria, Czechoslovakia, East Germany, Hungary, Poland, Romania, Soviet Union

NUMBER OF NUCLEAR WEAPONS IN THE LATE 1980s:

- U.S.: **23,000**
- Soviet Union: **39,000**

PEAK NUMBER OF NUCLEAR FALLOUT SHELTERS IN THE U.S.:

- About **200,000** in 1965

GLOSSARY

allies—countries that support and help other countries in a war

arms race—an event in which enemy countries try to build or collect weapons faster than the other can

communism—a social system in which property is controlled by the government

democracy—a system of government in which people choose the leaders

hydrogen bomb—a type of nuclear bomb

Iron Curtain—the political and military barrier that separated the Soviet Union and its allies from the rest of Europe during the Cold War

missiles—objects that are thrown or shot as weapons

nuclear weapons—very powerful weapons

protests—public events where people show disagreement with something

proxy wars—wars between two countries that are acting on behalf of more powerful countries; the more powerful countries do not fight each other directly.

Soviet Union—a country in eastern Europe and northern Asia from 1922 to 1991

tensions—states of being in which people or countries disagree with or feel anger toward each other

treaties—agreements between countries

Vietnam War—a conflict in Southeast Asia from 1954 to 1975

World War II—a conflict from 1939 to 1945 that involved many countries

TO LEARN MORE

AT THE LIBRARY

Huddleston, Emma. *How the Bomb Changed Everything.* Minneapolis, Minn.: Core Library, 2022.

Medina, Nico. *What Was the Berlin Wall?* New York, N.Y.: Penguin Workshop, 2019.

Monroe, Alex. *The Vietnam War.* Minneapolis, Minn.: Bellwether Media, 2024.

ON THE WEB

FACTSURFER

Factsurfer.com gives you a safe, fun way to find more information.

1. Go to www.factsurfer.com

2. Enter "Cold War" into the search box and click 🔍.

3. Select your book cover to see a list of related content.

INDEX

arms race, 8
Berlin Wall, 6, 7, 18, 19
by the numbers, 21
communism, 4, 6, 11
Cuba, 12, 13
Cuban Missile Crisis, 12, 13
democracy, 4, 17
East Germany, 6, 7, 18
Europe, 6, 11, 17, 18
Gorbachev, Mikhail, 16, 17, 20
hydrogen bomb, 9
Iron Curtain, 16
Kennedy, John F., 13
leaders, 13, 17
map, 5, 7
NATO, 5
nuclear weapons, 4, 8, 9, 11, 12, 13, 14, 20
protest, 11, 17, 18
proxy wars, 10
Soviet Union, 4, 5, 6, 8, 10, 11, 12, 13, 14, 15, 16, 18, 20
space race, 15
spies, 10, 12
Stalin, Joseph, 6
timeline, 18–19
treaties, 14
United States, 4, 5, 6, 8, 9, 10, 11, 12, 13, 14, 15, 16, 20
Vietnam War, 10
war at home, 11
Warsaw Pact, 5
West Germany, 6, 7, 18
World War II, 6

The images in this book are reproduced through the courtesy of: Colin Campbell/ Getty Images, cover (crowd); Bjoertvedt/ Wiki Commons, cover (guard towers); Florian-schäffer/ Wiki Commons, cover (Berlin Wall & city); Library of Congress Prints and Photographs Division Washington/ Library of Congress, cover (soldier on wall); ullstein bild/ Getty Images, pp. 2-3, 6-7, 22-23, 24; US Army Photo/ Alamy, pp. 4-5; U.S. Signal Corps photo uploaded and graphically created by Smiroje/ Wiki Commons, p. 6; Album/ Alamy, pp. 8, 18 (1949 entry); Photo Researchers/ Alamy, p. 9; byteboy/ Wiki Commons, p. 9 (bottom); Bettmann/ Getty Images, pp. 10, 14, 18 (1962 entry); Keystone-France/ Getty Images, p. 11; Everett Collection/ Alamy, p. 11 (bottom); RBM Vintage Images/ Alamy, p. 12; Cecil Stoughton. White House/ Wiki Commons, p. 13; NASA/ NASA, p. 15; The White House / Handout/ Getty Images, p. 16; Melde Press/Süddeutsche Zeitung Photo/ Alamy, p. 17; Sue Ream/ Wiki Commons, p. 19 (1989 entry); REUTERS PHOTOGRAPHER/ Alamy, pp. 20-21; High Contrast/ Wiki Commons, back cover.